SACRAMENTO PUBLIC LIBRARY
828 "I" STREET
SACRAMENTO, CA 95814

7/2009

D0574954

Airplanes Inside and Out

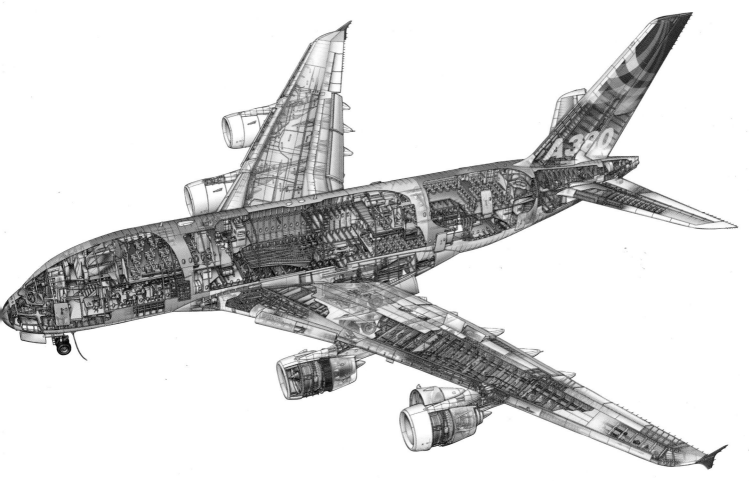

Chris Oxlade

PowerKiDS
press

New York

Published in 2009 by The Rosen Publishing Group Inc.
29 East 21st Street, New York, NY 10010

Copyright © 2009 Wayland/The Rosen Publishing Group, Inc.

All rights reserved. No part of this book may be reproduced in any
form without permission from the publisher, except by a reviewer.

First Edition

Senior Editor: Jennifer Schofield
Editor: Rob Scott Colson
Designer: Darren Jordan
Consultant: Ben Russell

Library of Congress Cataloging-in-Publication Data

Oxlade, Chris.
Airplanes inside and out / Chris Oxlade. — 1st ed.
    p. cm. — (Machines inside out)
Includes bibliographical references and index.
ISBN 978-1-4358-2863-6 (library binding)
ISBN 978-1-4358-2941-1 (paperback)
ISBN 978-1-4358-2945-9 (6-pack)
1. Airplanes—Parts—Juvenile literature. 2. Airplanes—Equipment and supplies—
Juvenile literature. 3. Airplanes--Juvenile literature. I. Title.
TL547.0943 2009
629.134--dc22
                            2008026174

Manufactured in China

Acknowledgments
Cover Ramon Berk/istockphoto, 2007 The Flight Collection/www.theflightcollection.com.
6–7 2007 The Flight Collection/www.theflightcollection.com, 8–9 2007 The Flight Collection/www.theflightcollection.com,
8 IABG, 9 J. Schwanke/Dreamstime.com, 10–11 2007 The Flight Collection/www.theflightcollection.com,
10 Joegough/Dreamstime.com, 11 Jose Manuel Gelpi Diaz/Dreamstime.com, 12–13 2007 The Flight Collection/
www.theflightcollection.com, 13t Brian Grant/Dreamstime.com, 13b Chris Fourie/Dreamstime.com , 14–15 2007
The Flight Collection/www.theflightcollection.com, 14 Frederic Fahraeus/Dreamstime.com, 15 David Monniaux, 16t
Cb34inc/Dreamstime.com, 16b Lockheed Martin, 17 Lockheed Martin, 18–19 Airbus, 18 Arpingstone, 19 Collosos/
GNU, 20–21 2007 The Flight Collection/www.theflightcollection.com, 20 Andres Rodriguez/Dreamstime.com, 21
Kirill Zdorov/Dreamstime.com, 22 Justin Lane/epa/Corbis, 23 2007 The Flight Collection/www.theflightcollection.com,
24–25 Stephen Sweet/Dreamstime.com, 25l Thinkstock/Corbis, 25r US Air Force, 26–27 2007 The Flight
Collection/www.theflightcollection.com, 27t Chris Fourie/Dreamstime.com, 27b Nicholas Rjabow/Dreamstime.com

Contents

Planes inside out

An airplane is an amazingly complex machine. It is made up of thousands of parts, from tiny electronic components in the cockpit, to giant pieces of metal in the wings. This plane is an Airbus A380, which is the world's largest airliner. It is 240 feet (73 meters) long and 262 feet (80 meters) across. This illustration shows its major parts.

Fuselage
This is the main part of the aircraft, and where the passengers sit. The tubular frame has a skin made of metal.

Cockpit
This is where the pilots sit. It contains flying controls, computers, and other electronic instruments that help the pilots to fly and navigate the aircraft.

Landing gear
The landing gear lets the plane roll along the ground. There are five sets of wheels under the fuselage or wings and under the nose.

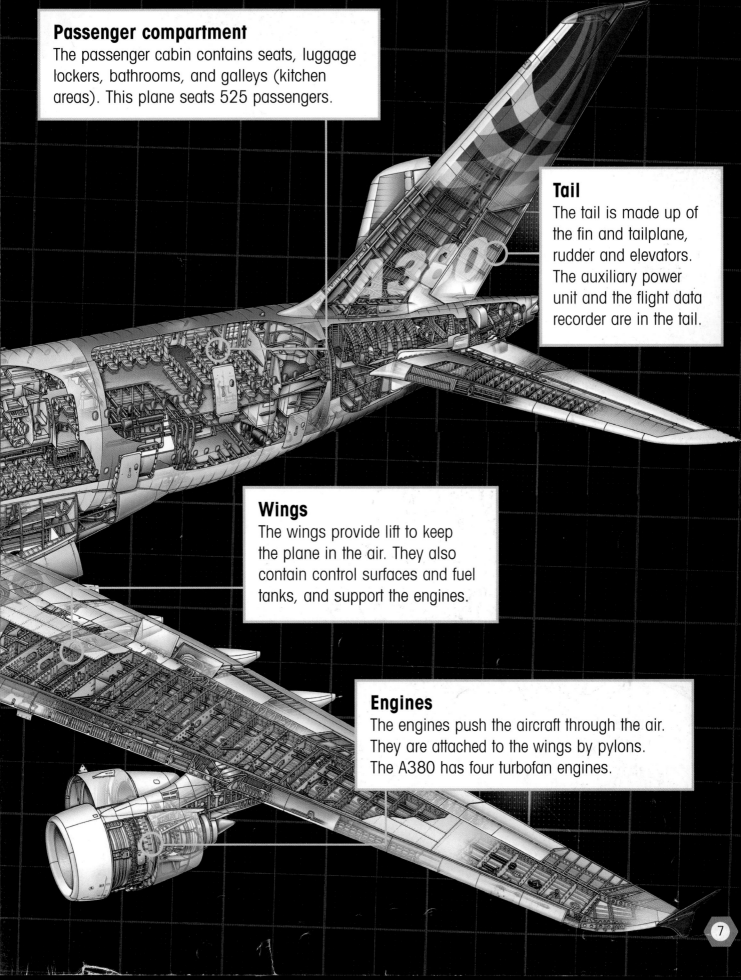

Passenger compartment
The passenger cabin contains seats, luggage lockers, bathrooms, and galleys (kitchen areas). This plane seats 525 passengers.

Tail
The tail is made up of the fin and tailplane, rudder and elevators. The auxiliary power unit and the flight data recorder are in the tail.

Wings
The wings provide lift to keep the plane in the air. They also contain control surfaces and fuel tanks, and support the engines.

Engines
The engines push the aircraft through the air. They are attached to the wings by pylons. The A380 has four turbofan engines.

Fuselage structure

This plane has a semimonocoque fuselage. This means that the fuselage of an airliner is a tube, which is a very strong shape. It is often made up of a metal skin on top of a metal frame. Modern aircraft are made from advanced materials called composites, such as glass-fiber and carbon-fiber reinforced plastic. These are stronger and lighter than metals.

Skin

Frames, stringers, and skin

The internal frame is made up of hoops called ribs around the fuselage and rods, called stringers, along the fuselage. The skin is attached to the outside of the frame. The two passenger decks and the cargo deck make the fuselage even stronger.

Aircraft construction

In an aircraft factory, the fuselage is made in giant sections. The sections are then joined end to end to make up the finished fuselage. This is one of the sections that make up an Airbus A380 fuselage.

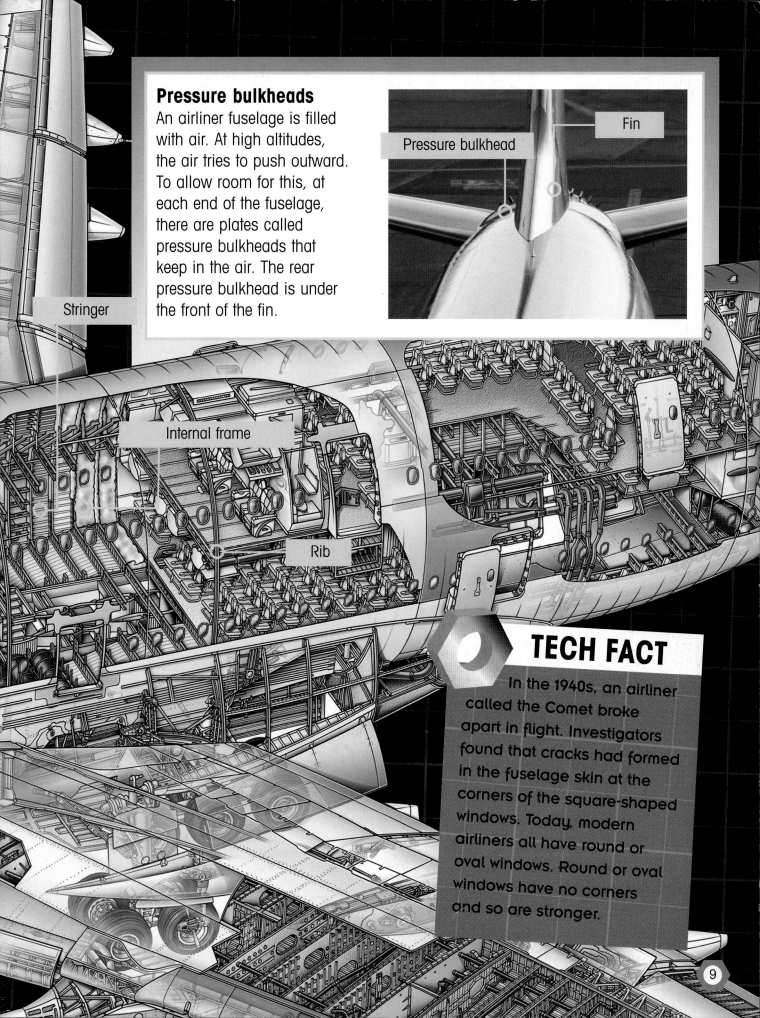

Pressure bulkheads

An airliner fuselage is filled with air. At high altitudes, the air tries to push outward. To allow room for this, at each end of the fuselage, there are plates called pressure bulkheads that keep in the air. The rear pressure bulkhead is under the front of the fin.

Pressure bulkhead

Fin

Stringer

Internal frame

Rib

TECH FACT

In the 1940s, an airliner called the Comet broke apart in flight. Investigators found that cracks had formed in the fuselage skin at the corners of the square-shaped windows. Today, modern airliners all have round or oval windows. Round or oval windows have no corners and so are stronger.

Flying surfaces

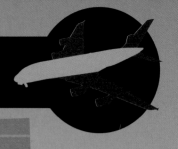

The wings and tail of an aircraft are called its flying surfaces. As the aircraft flies through the air, the wings make an upward force, called lift. This lift supports the aircraft. The tail is made up of the vertical fin and the horizontal tailplane. It keeps the aircraft flying straight and level. The wings are extremely strong. On the ground, they support the weight of the engines.

Inside a wing

A wing is formed of a frame covered with a skin. The frame is made up of spars that run along the length of the wing, and ribs that go from front to back. There are usually two spars, a front spar and a rear spar, although some large, modern airplanes have three. The spars and ribs form the sides of boxes inside the wing, called wing boxes. Some of these boxes are used as fuel tanks.

TECH FACT

Although wings are very strong, they can bend upward and downward. On the ground, the wings bend down because they are holding up the engines. In flight, they bend upward, because they are holding up the fuselage. The tip of a large wing can bend more than 23 feet (7 meters).

Tailplane structure

The structure of the fin and the tailplane is similar to that of the wings. Inside are spars and ribs, and outside is a skin of metal. The rudder and ailerons are made of lightweight materials and are moved by hydraulic rams called actuators.

Fin

Tailplane

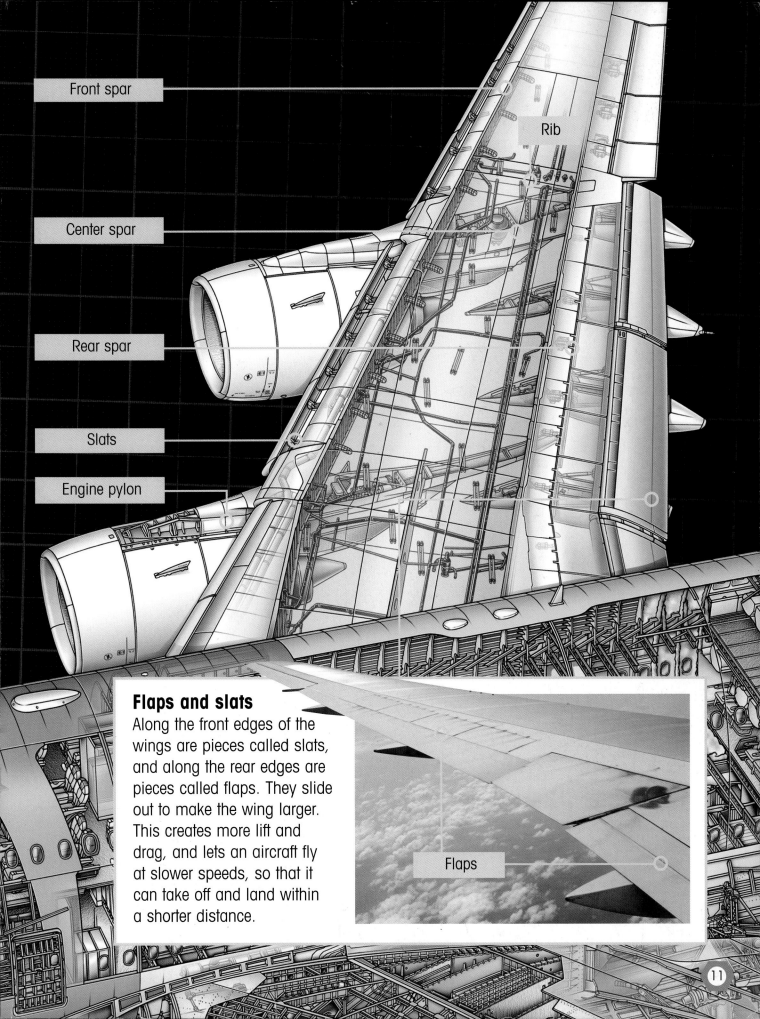

Front spar

Rib

Center spar

Rear spar

Slats

Engine pylon

Flaps and slats

Along the front edges of the wings are pieces called slats, and along the rear edges are pieces called flaps. They slide out to make the wing larger. This creates more lift and drag, and lets an aircraft fly at slower speeds, so that it can take off and land within a shorter distance.

Flaps

Turbofan engines

Engines push an aircraft through the air. They push air and other gases backward, and this pushes the aircraft forward. The push they produce is called thrust. There are several different types of aircraft engine. Large airliners, business jets, and large transport aircraft use a type of jet engine called a turbofan.

How a turbofan works

Some of the air that enters the engine goes into the compressor, and then into the combustion chamber. The air allows fuel to burn in the combustion chamber, to make hot gases that drive the turbine.

TECH FACT

Some parts of a turbofan turbine spin more than 200 times a second. The temperature inside the engine can reach more than 1,832°F (1.000°C) and so turbofans are built with special materials that will not melt. The parts are tested to make sure the turbofan will not break if a bird flies into it.

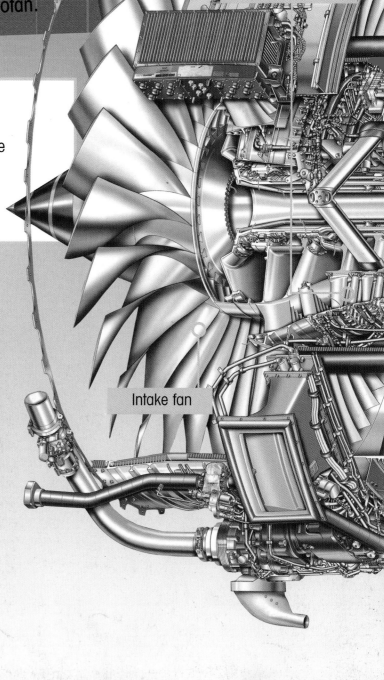

Compressor squeezes air

Intake fan

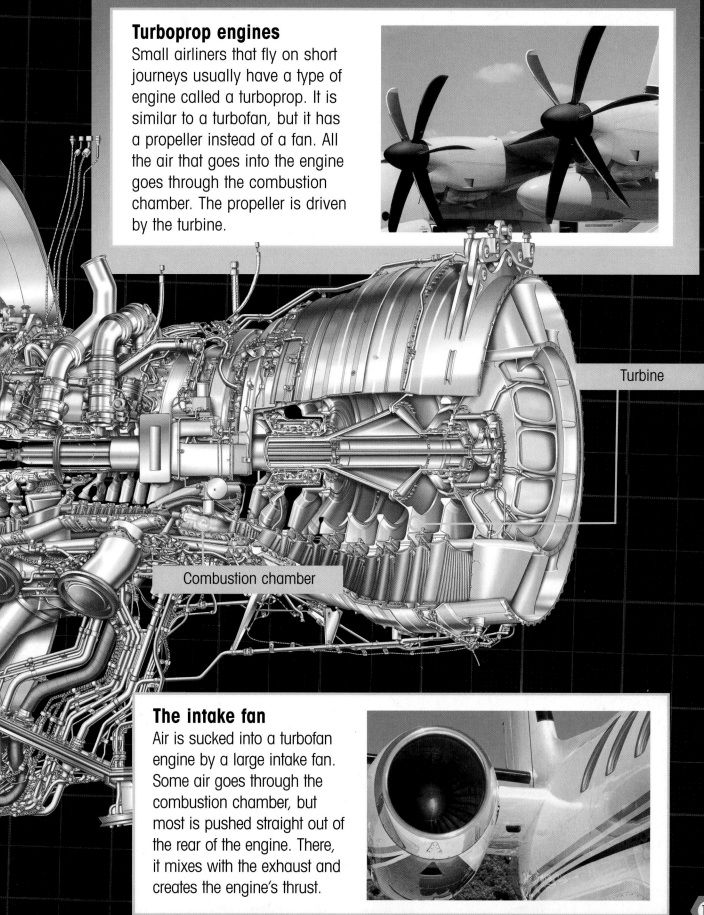

Turboprop engines

Small airliners that fly on short journeys usually have a type of engine called a turboprop. It is similar to a turbofan, but it has a propeller instead of a fan. All the air that goes into the engine goes through the combustion chamber. The propeller is driven by the turbine.

Turbine

Combustion chamber

The intake fan

Air is sucked into a turbofan engine by a large intake fan. Some air goes through the combustion chamber, but most is pushed straight out of the rear of the engine. There, it mixes with the exhaust and creates the engine's thrust.

Servicing and fueling

A jet engine needs many extra parts to keep it working. For example, it needs pipes and pumps to take fuel to the combustion chamber, and oil to keep the parts moving smoothly. Most turbofan engines also have thrust reversers, which are used on landing. They fold out and deflect the jet exhaust forward, slowing the aircraft down.

Engine servicing

Just like a car engine, an aircraft engine must be carefully looked after so that it keeps working properly and does not break down. Inspection covers open up to let engineers look at the insides of the engine. If an engine breaks down and cannot be fixed, it is changed for a new one.

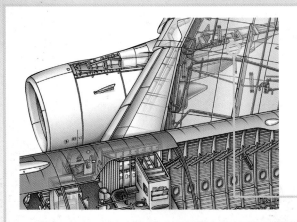

Engine fuel

Turbofan engines and other jet engines use a special type of fuel called aviation fuel. The most common aviation fuel is called JET A-1. On an airliner, the fuel is stored in tanks inside the wings. It is pumped into the wings from a fuel tanker or underground storage tanks.

Fuel tank

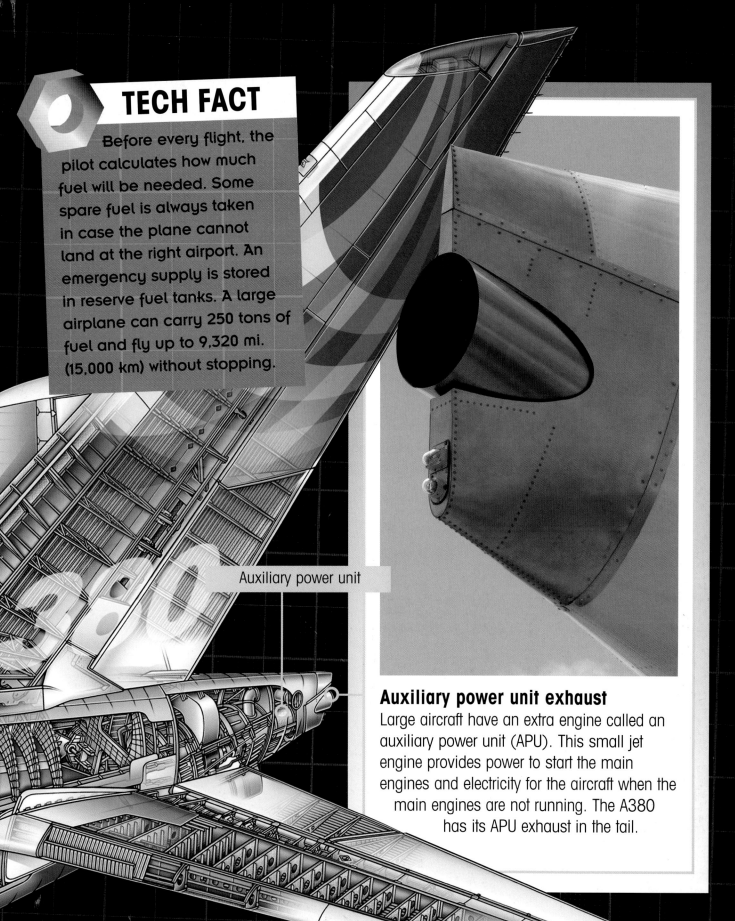

TECH FACT

Before every flight, the pilot calculates how much fuel will be needed. Some spare fuel is always taken in case the plane cannot land at the right airport. An emergency supply is stored in reserve fuel tanks. A large airplane can carry 250 tons of fuel and fly up to 9,320 mi. (15,000 km) without stopping.

Auxiliary power unit

Auxiliary power unit exhaust

Large aircraft have an extra engine called an auxiliary power unit (APU). This small jet engine provides power to start the main engines and electricity for the aircraft when the main engines are not running. The A380 has its APU exhaust in the tail.

Military jet engines

Combat aircraft are also powered by jet engines. Most of them have turbofans, like airliners, but a few have turbojets instead. These jet engines do not have a large fan like a turbofan. One or two engines are placed inside or underneath the fuselage. This lets the aircraft roll quickly from side to side, so it can make quick turns to attack enemy planes or make an escape.

Thrust and weight
Combat aircraft such as this F-18 need to accelerate and climb quickly, so they have very powerful engines. Most modern fighters have engines that produce more thrust than their own weight. With engines on full power, they can climb straight up.

Afterburners
The glow at the back of this fighter comes from its afterburner. Here, fuel is injected into the hot exhaust gases from the engine. The fuel burns, producing more hot gases and extra thrust. Pilots use their afterburners in short bursts for quick takeoffs and fast climbs.

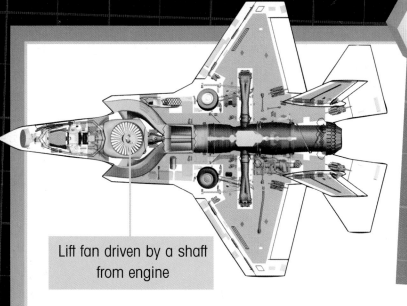

It would be impossible for the pilot to fly the F-35B without the help of on-board computers. In vertical flight, the computers control the thrust from each of the nozzles and the lift fan. Very accurate control is essential to keep the aircraft from flipping over.

Lift fan driven by a shaft from engine

Vertical flight

The Lockheed Martin F-35B is a short takeoff and vertical landing (STOVL) combat aircraft. The engine produces forward thrust for normal flight and downward thrust for takeoff and vertical landings. For vertical landings, the rear nozzle bends to point downward. The engine exhaust comes from the rear nozzle and from two small nozzles under the wings. More vertical thrust comes from the lift fan behind the cockpit.

Doors open to allow air into the lift fan

Landing gear

All aircraft need landing gear (also called undercarriage) for takeoff and landing. The main landing gear of most modern aircraft is under the wings or fuselage, and a nose wheel under the nose. This is known as a tricycle undercarriage. During flight, the landing gear retracts (folds away) into landing gear compartments, which are covered with folding doors.

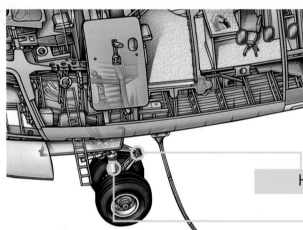

Struts and locks

The landing gear wheels are on the end of sturdy legs. The legs are raised and lowered by hydraulic rams. Struts lock the legs in place to stop them from wobbling. There are shock absorbers inside the legs to soak up bumps when the aircraft lands.

Hydraulic rams

Shock absorbers

Ready to land

A pilot lowers the landing gear a few minutes before an aircraft lands. The legs fold down and lock into place. Indicator lights in the cockpit will then show that the landing gear is properly down. This Boeing 747 has four sets of main wheels. On the ground, the nose wheel is used to steer the aircraft.

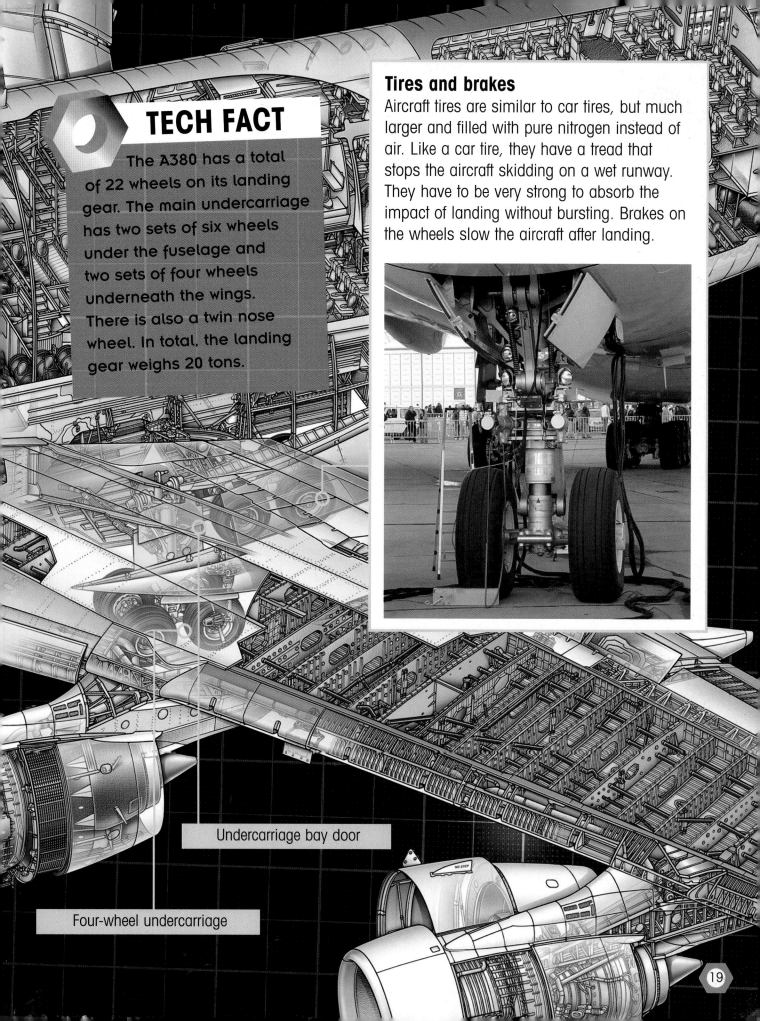

TECH FACT

The A380 has a total of 22 wheels on its landing gear. The main undercarriage has two sets of six wheels under the fuselage and two sets of four wheels underneath the wings. There is also a twin nose wheel. In total, the landing gear weighs 20 tons.

Tires and brakes

Aircraft tires are similar to car tires, but much larger and filled with pure nitrogen instead of air. Like a car tire, they have a tread that stops the aircraft skidding on a wet runway. They have to be very strong to absorb the impact of landing without bursting. Brakes on the wheels slow the aircraft after landing.

Undercarriage bay door

Four-wheel undercarriage

Inside the fuselage

Inside an aircraft's fuselage is a large, empty space. In an airliner, the space forms the passenger cabin. It is filled with seats for passengers, bathrooms, and galleys, where the crew stores and prepares food. Under the cabin is a cargo hold for the passengers' baggage. A superjumbo like the A380 has two full-length decks in the passenger cabin.

Cabin services

An airliner cabin contains services that passengers need for comfort and entertainment on long flights. These include lighting, video screens, wireless computer networks, and bathrooms. Cables and pipes hidden behind panels carry electricity, signals, and water through the aircraft.

Seating

An airliner can have different arrangements of seats. The type and number of seats, and how far they are from each other, can all be changed. The normal layout for the A380 is 525 seats, but it has a maximum capacity of 853 seats.

Business-class seating

First-class seating

Economy seating

Overhead lockers

Rear stairs

TECH FACT

Pressurization

Jet-powered airliners cruise at an altitude of about 32,800 ft. (10,000 m). This high up, the air is too thin to breathe. An airliner fuselage is filled with air for passengers to breathe. This is called cabin pressurization. The air is pumped into the cabin along air-conditioning ducts.

Cargo hold

The cargo hold of an airliner is at the bottom of the fuselage. It has its own large doors for passenger baggage and other cargo to be loaded and unloaded. On larger airliners, the baggage is packed into cargo containers that fit snugly into the cargo hold.

Flight deck and controls

The flight deck is the area at the front of the fuselage where the pilots sit. There are usually two seats side by side on the flight deck. They are surrounded by controls for flying and for operating the aircraft's systems. There are also lights, dials, and screens that show information about the aircraft.

Flying controls

The pilots' main flying controls are the control column and rudder pedals. They move hinged control surfaces, the ailerons on the wings, the elevators on the tailplane, and the rudder on the fin. These surfaces make the aircraft turn, climb, or descend. In the nose of the aircraft are computers and other electronics, called avionics, which help the pilots to fly and navigate, such as the autopilot.

TECH FACT

Most modern airliners, including the Airbus A380, have a flight control system called fly by wire. This means that a computer is in control of the ailerons, elevators, rudder, and engines. The pilot decides when to turn, climb, or descend, but the computer flies the aircraft.

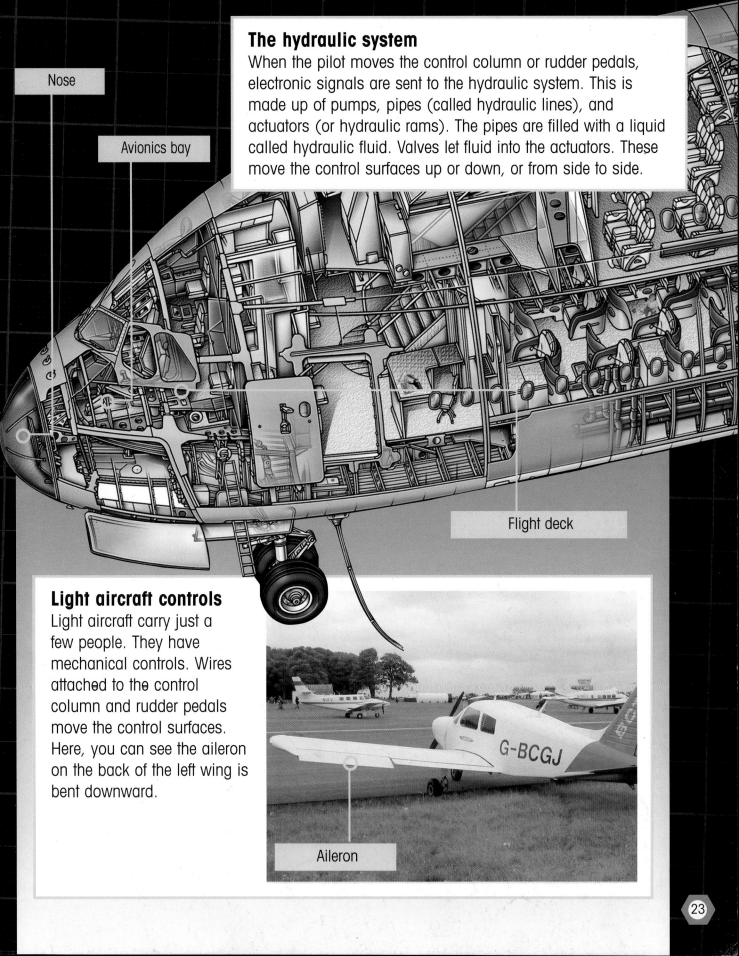

Nose

Avionics bay

The hydraulic system

When the pilot moves the control column or rudder pedals, electronic signals are sent to the hydraulic system. This is made up of pumps, pipes (called hydraulic lines), and actuators (or hydraulic rams). The pipes are filled with a liquid called hydraulic fluid. Valves let fluid into the actuators. These move the control surfaces up or down, or from side to side.

Flight deck

Light aircraft controls

Light aircraft carry just a few people. They have mechanical controls. Wires attached to the control column and rudder pedals move the control surfaces. Here, you can see the aileron on the back of the left wing is bent downward.

G-BCGJ

Aileron

Emergency!

Aircraft such as the A380 are very safe. Even so, they have many parts that help the crew and passengers in case of an emergency. These include oxygen masks, emergency lights, and escape slides. There are also systems that stop pilots from making mistakes. For example, the ground proximity warning sounds an alarm if the aircraft flies too low.

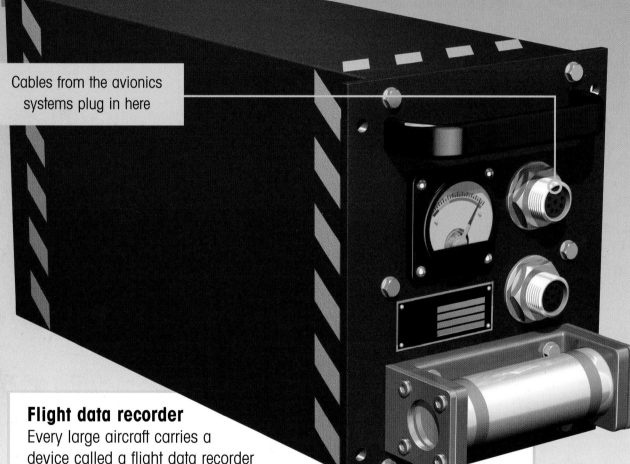

Cables from the avionics systems plug in here

Flight data recorder
Every large aircraft carries a device called a flight data recorder (FDR), nicknamed the "black box." It records details about a flight, such as altitude and speed, and what the pilots are saying to each other. The FDR is in a strong metal container in the aircraft's tail. If an aircraft crash-lands, the information from the FDR helps investigators to find out what happened in the moments before the accident.

TECH FACT

In an emergency landing, an aircraft usually loses electrical power. This can leave the cabin in darkness, so there are lines of battery-powered colored lights in the cabin floor that show the way to the emergency exits.

Ejection seats

In a combat aircraft, the pilot sits in an ejection seat. If the aircraft is going to crash, the pilot pulls a handle and the seat blasts out of the cockpit. First, the cockpit's glass canopy is released and flies into the air. Then small rockets fire the seat upward. When the seat is clear of the aircraft, a parachute comes out and the seat floats to the ground. It takes less than a second for the pilot to be ejected.

Cabin equipment

There is an oxygen mask above each seat in the cabin. If the cabin air pressure falls at high altitude, the masks drop down, giving passengers oxygen so that they can breathe. There are life jackets under each seat in case the aircraft has to land in water. The cabin doors contain inflatable escape slides and life rafts.

Helicopter parts

On the inside of a helicopter are some parts that are similar to an airliner, and some parts that are very different. The structure of the fuselage is like an airliner, with a metal frame covered with a skin. Inside are seats, a cockpit, and avionics. The main difference is that the engines are on top of the fuselage. They drive a rotor that lifts the helicopter into the air.

Flying controls

These are the cyclic pitch control, the collective pitch control, and the rudder pedals. The cyclic control makes the helicopter move forward, backward, or sideways. The collective control makes it climb or descend. The rudder pedals make it turn left or right.

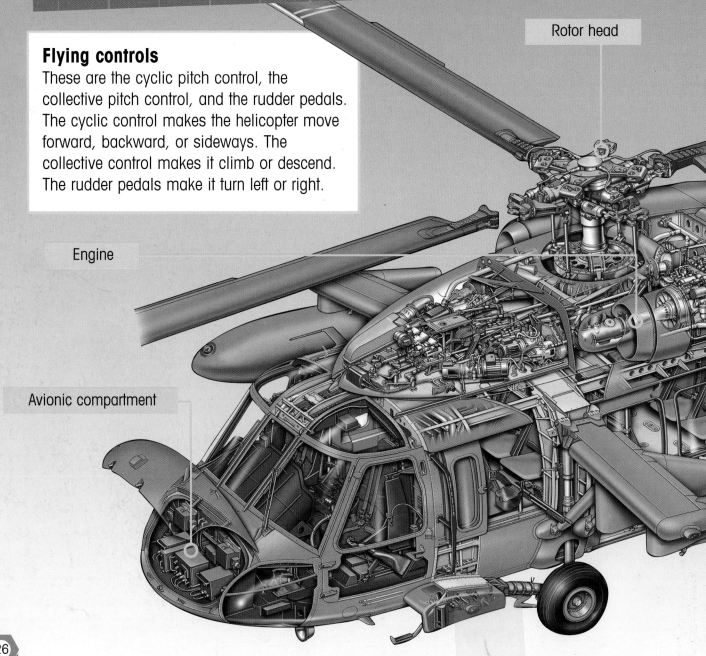

Rotor head

Engine

Avionic compartment

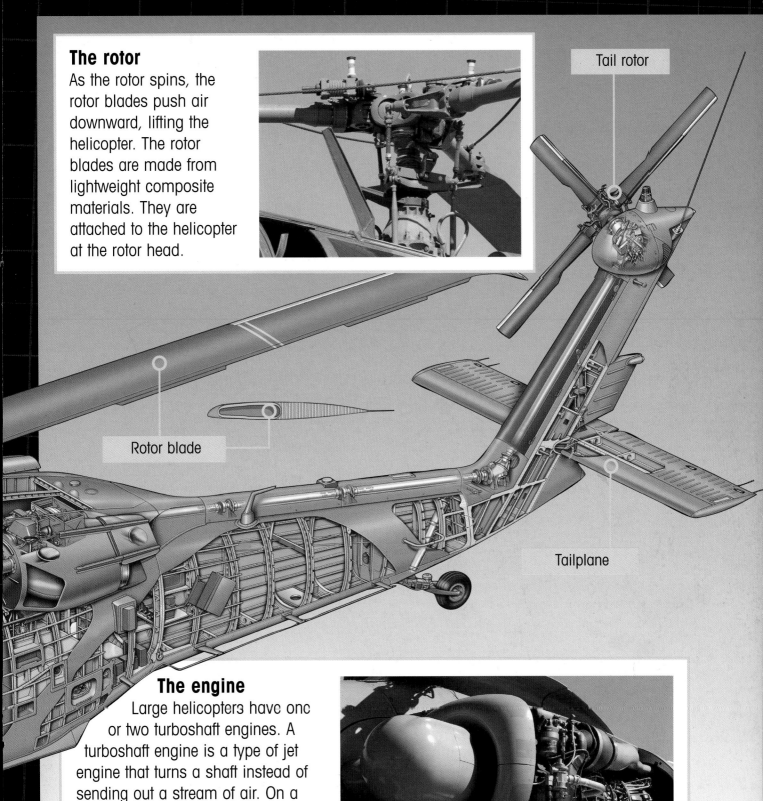

The rotor

As the rotor spins, the rotor blades push air downward, lifting the helicopter. The rotor blades are made from lightweight composite materials. They are attached to the helicopter at the rotor head.

Tail rotor

Rotor blade

Tailplane

The engine

Large helicopters have one or two turboshaft engines. A turboshaft engine is a type of jet engine that turns a shaft instead of sending out a stream of air. On a helicopter, the shaft turns the main rotor and the tail rotor. The tail rotor makes a sideways push that stops the fuselage from spinning the opposite way to the main rotor.

Glossary

Aileron
A control surface on the rear edge of a wing.

Altitude
A measure of height above sea level.

Auxiliary power unit (APU)
A small engine that produces electricity for an aircraft's systems when the main engines are switched off.

Avionics
The electronics that help a pilot to fly and navigate an aircraft.

Carbon-fiber reinforced plastic
A composite material made by embedding thin fibers of pure carbon in hard plastic.

Cockpit
The area where pilots sit to fly an aircraft.

Component
An object that is part of a larger, more complex machine.

Composite material
A material made by combining two other materials, giving it better properties than either of them alone.

Compressor
A machine that squeezes (compresses) air.

Control surface
A hinged section of an aircraft's wings and tailplane, used to steer the aircraft through the air.

Duct
A pipe used to move air around an aircraft or a building.

Elevator
A control surface on the rear edge of the tailplane, which makes the plane climb or descend.

Fin
The vertical section of the tail at the back of an aircraft. Also known as the vertical stabilizer.

Flight data recorder
A device that records the details of an aircraft's flight. The data can be used to help find the cause of any accident.

Fuselage
The main part of an aircraft, where the pilots and passengers sit, and where cargo is carried.

Glass-fiber reinforced plastic
A composite material made by embedding glass fibers in hard plastic.

Hydraulic
Describes a machine that has parts moved by liquid pumped along pipes.

Hydraulic ram
A cylinder with a piston that is pushed in or out by pumped liquid.

Landing gear
Wheels that let an aircraft roll along on the ground.

Navigate
Find the way from one place to another.

Nose
The very front of an aircraft's fuselage.

Rudder
A control surface on the rear edge of the fin.

Turbine
A device that spins when gases flow through it.

Turbofan
A type of jet engine used on most large modern airliners. It has a large intake fan at the front.

Further reading

The Need for Speed: Aircraft
by Christopher Maynard
(LernerSports, 1999)

Extreme Machines: Planes
by David Jefferis
(Smart Apple Media, 2007)

The World's Greatest Warplanes
by Ian Graham
(Raintree, 2005)

Web Sites

Due to the changing nature of Internet links, PowerKids Press has developed an online list of Web sites related to the subject of this book. This site is updated regularly. Please use this link to access this list:
www.powerkidslinks.com/mio/airplane

Index